Highways Feelings

Poetry of all types

By

Paul Randall Fox © Highway

Copyright

Dedication:

All readers who love poetry

Introduction:

This book contains poetry, of all types.

Index:

Broken Heart

Nature at its Best

Senses

Peace

Alive Again

Beauty of Creation

Passion

First Sight

Mothers Smile

Words of Silence

Conflicts

Snow

BBQ

Her Love

As she walked up to me

My heart was racing as the sea

Her eyes

Oh

How majestic they are as she looks at me

Her smile

As beautiful as the glorious sunset

On an open sea

Her touch is as soft

Like a bed of rose pebbles can only be

Her fragrance as sweet

As the lily's in a summer night breeze

Her soft kiss

Was gently sweet and moist

As a honey from a tree

My nerves were calmed

As she hugs me

As close as we could be

She tames my heart out of love

For it is truly what I want it to be

She gives herself freely

For its only to me

My life is full for she gave it to me

My love for her will always be

For she is the beauty in my heart

That will never leave

For I smile knowing she truly loves me

Black Rose

As my tears roll down my cheeks

I look beyond in disbelief

The beauty she holds

Grabs my heart should it be told

As she waves back and forth

I fall for her as before

As she sings with the breeze

You hear her beat

With the sound of the waterfalls

Pinging against the stone walls

How majestic she can be

As the sunset sets

Below the trees

For that moment

I believe

It is the most beautiful thing

I have ever seen

One single black rose

Between the mountain trees

Beauty of Morning

As I smell the aroma

Of the fresh ground coffee

I watch her

walking through the kitchen bare

I gander upon her beauty

For she is truly perfect

Everywhere

Her long red silky hair

As it waves to me

While she stares into my eyes

So I can see

The hair was nicely braded

Just for me

It brings a color to her smile

Which I want to see

She looks my way

She brings grace

To me every day

Those beautiful green eyes

I can see

As she slowly walks

Across the floor

Towards me

For that gentle moment

When we meet

Our lips

Touch so blissfully

For they are sweet

As the honey from a tree

My heart pounds vigorously

For I feel her heart

Catching me

As she slowly wraps her arms

Around my neck

I cannot help

But to pull her closer

For we both want to kiss

The smile upon her face

Makes me happy

This is truly an excellent day

I do not want to miss

The Reaper Lost

I lay here silently

Waiting to see

What the pain has in store for me

Pain is my friend I must say

For we live together every day

Again and again

I play the game

Facing the death

That cancer brings

I beat the reaper at his game

Denying the honor

Which the reaper will gain

Time after time

I go and see

All the doctors

Making a fuss over me

Each time that I leave

They are all amazed at me

Now I sit here writing away

Hoping to have more time

To say what I came to say

Living day by day

I tell what I feel

Only hoping

That I will never fail

Pain is my friend I must say

For we live together every day

My minds clear

As to what I want to say

Only my feelings run astray

Soon enough it will be

The final moment for me

Whether I lose the game

Or live to have a ripe old age

Final Goodbye

My eyes

See over the sea

The majestic beauty

The moonlight gives to me

As the waves ripple slowly to me

I taste the salt from the open sea

I put my final goodbye

In a bottle wrapped in pink

I remember

I can see her face

As I toss it into the sea

Remembering how much

She truly loved me

Now

I have nowhere to go

For my heart is now cold

Angry at what I have lost

I do not care

What others may think

For my heart feels cheated

And in disbelief

One moment we are wild and free

And as happy as we can be

Then we spent what time we had left

Fighting the cancer

Both of us regret

My love for her will never die

For I have already

Said my goodbye

As my tears

Rolled from my eyes

FOR HIM

I walk through the paths

In the mountain sides

Slowly walking

In small strides

Gazing upon the night skies

Wondering

What will be for me

When the morning dew

Set's nature free

Upon the stone I sit

Trying to get my life

In my mind to fit

Confusing

It can be for me

For all I wanted

Was you to be with me

Now I know

How cold it can be

For your love

Was for him

Not me

Love of Night

I lay here in silence

Upon the cold ground

Hearing only that

Which nature offers in sound

While I gazed upon her beauty

It brought joy

And calms to my heart

Her radiant smile of light

Lay upon my chest

Throughout the night

This brought warmth to my soul

Which is wrapped

Around my heart

As the night passes us by

She sheds her tears

Which add light to the night sky

I watch her tears

Gracefully fade away

As her smile slips away

Hoping

The night

Would never go away

Portals of Love

My desire

Is to see

All that is majestic

To the heart and the eyes for me

Is this the very essence

Of beauty I see

Which brings joy - peace - love to me

Precious Moments

Precious moments of the mind

Kindly leave us behind

The joy of kindness

In one's heart to see

Is it the love

In one's heart can only be

Only the heart

Can bring a new start

As if it were spring from the start

True Love

I walk upon the beach

Wearing nothing on my feet

While the breeze blows thru

And the sunset begins

My longing for your love

Is strong once again

I canter that moment

Of when we walked hand in hand

The gentleness of your voice

Was soft as the sand

In that final moment

When kissed our final good bye

Made my heartache

For it brought tears to my eyes

I know now

That you are in a better place

I know this to be true

My heart

Will always be for you

Heart on Fire

When we met

Our hearts did connect

All my dreams of you

I kept

As we walked about the land

We walked hand in hand

This made me feel loved

Again and again

When you smile at me

I can see our family tree

You put my heart on fire

For it is you

My heart desires

Years have gone by

To my surprise

Our love together

Has made us wise

The value of our hearts

We cannot disguise

For everyone sees how true you are to me

For it's like being on a sailboat

Crossing the sea

It's a never-ending journey

For it was meant to be

As we walk down the aisle

To say I do

We knew our hearts

are one in one

And a hundred percent true

Now we're here

For many years

With three children who gave us cheers

Now were getting older

As we lay our heads

On each other's shoulders

Sitting by the fire

For it's our heart desire

We have

A wonderful relationship

That will never expire

For we both know

Our hearts

Are on fire

Grace

Waking up everyday

You know you have been graced with life

When you walk into your kitchen

She walks up to you and hugs you tight

You have been graced with her love

When you walk about the land

Holding one another's hands

You have been graced by Nature

When your home sitting by the fire

You have been graced with warmth

While you are reading a good book

You know you have been graced with knowledge

When she sits in your lap by the warm fire

A smile she gives to you

You know you have graced

Grace

Enjoy life

No matter where you are

Or what you may have

Life has given you grace

Broken Heart

My heart is sad

It cannot be glad

I have no way to be happy in this day

My mind feels the past

But it cannot let me pass

As I seek a way to go

My soul will not let go

It saddens my heart to believe

That you are gone from me

My love was happy and rich

With the touch of your gentle kiss

When we took our walks

Through the hills

I kept you warm

So you would not get chills

Now I lay here to sleep

My body aches in disbelief

I cannot understand why

I have lost such love

And could not say goodbye

I search for you every day

Hoping for the chance to say

That I miss you with all my heart

Then the tears begin to start

I lay a red rose

Upon your grave

My heart aches

As it turns cold and grey

Only then

I realize the cost

Which leaves me broken hearted

For what I've lost

Nature at its Best

I watch the clouds

Roll back and forth

As they run into one another

Releasing their fury upon the ground

While the clouds roar

The ground shakes

The wind blows

The rain follows the wind

Softly pinging upon the land

The trees begin to sway

With drops of rain upon their leaves

Soothing to the ears and eyes

You breath the crisp clean air

Your mind begins to ponder in thought

Admiring nature for its abilities

Bringing fury – peace

Throughout the land

Senses

Laying upon the fields

In a distance you can hear

Natures music in your ears

So peaceful you close your eyes

To relax the strain on your mind

The gentle breeze

Brings goosebumps on your arms

Your smile shows

The wonderful sensation you feel

A pleasing moment in time

Which brings pleasure to your body and mind

Peace

This is truly the desire of one

Everyone wants peace and love

Sensuality

The simplicity of life

We all know that life

A life that is free

What we have in life

Is what we make it to be

The true essence of free will

Is finding out

Were you want to be

Here I sit

Pondering upon my past

Looking at

Where I am present and past

In my life knowing

That I have given all I could

Should the opportunity arise

You know where I will be

Looking upon the valley below

With a happy heart

Full of love

ALIVE AGAIN

As we ponder upon our thoughts

We are reminded of our hearts

For the love that we give

A sensual and precious gift it is

We open our hearts

As much as we can

Only wanting

To feel alive again

BEAUTY OF CREATION

To know that

Which is beautiful

Is to understand

That which was given freely to all

The majestic beauty

Of our creation

Is soothing to the eyes and soul

The hand you extend

Must be that of warmth and love to begin

Always be true

To thyself and the world

Passion

To seek that

which you do not understand

can it be passion

Is it truly the passion

That we seek

Is passion the pathway

To wisdom that we seek

If so

Then wisdom

Becomes your teacher

Hand in Hand

The color of her eyes

were like crystal blue sea

Her smile

Is as beautiful

As a majestic mountain scene

The hands

Are as gentle as silk against your skin

Her lips

are as moist

As a soft drizzle

Upon the land

Dreaming someday

We can walk hand in hand

A pleasant dream in my mind

That will never end

To have that

That cannot be

Is a pain in the heart

That no one can see

Which can be

As traumatic as the storms

In the rough open seas

First Sight

To know that

Which troubles your heart

It was there from the start

When your eyes locked with one another

Your hearts

Began to flutter

Only then

Did you realize

That it was love at first sight

Now you cannot think

Of anything else

But about one another

Which cannot be helped

As you sit by the fire

It's both of your heart's desire

As you hold each other's hands

That's when you both understand

That this relationship

Will never end

Mother Smile

As I took my first breath

I was cold and wet

I could not see

But I feel your smile upon me

I did not know

What was to be

Just that my mother

Truly loved me

As I grew up I could see

My mother

Was always there for me

It broke my heart and made me sad to see

My mother's heart

When I had to leave

Every time

I came home to see

My mother

Welcomed me

With open arms

A mother's smile and love can be

Like a snow-white dove

Flying above me

So I am grateful you see

For I know

That my mother truly loves me

On her special days

Always remember to say

How much your life means to you every day

Give her a hug

That really shows her love

Then you both will know

What it's like

To be loved

Words of Silence

In a distance

I see her tears

Rolling down her cheeks

As I ponder the thought

Of what could have brought such distraught

For her beauty I see

Is as eloquent as a princess should be

Yet I see

The sadness while she sits on her knees

I am angered for what I see

Such destruction to beauty

Cannot be

As I approach her slowly

She looks upon me

With a broken heart

Which I can see

I extend my arms as she comes to me

Embracing her gently and holding her tight

In hopes she will feel

Warm and secure through her plight

Time passes us by gracefully

As she gathers herself so eloquently

As she looked into my eyes

I can see her heart

Then she turns

And walks away

Her smile was adequate thanks

I am very pleased to see

A happy princess walk away from me

Lost

You close your eyes

While you are sleeping

You begin a journey

In your dreams

You are mumbling words in your sleep

A few seconds past

You wake up abruptly

Sitting on your bed

Not remembering what was in your head

Feeling lost sitting on your bed

Conflicts

Mind – Body – Soul

All in a world of its own

Isolation can be

Robust and harsh to me

When your conflict starts

The war within

Battles with body-mind-soul

Looking for answers

Which you do not know

In the end there will be

Harmony and peace

For the body and mind

The victory given within your soul

Which made you let it all go

Snow

I look out my window

A surprise to me

The ground covered in a blanket of white

Snow is falling blissfully through the night

Each flake is unique on its own

All different shapes when they fall to the ground

Children across the way

Begin to play

Building snowman's and more

On the hill the other way

I watch children riding their sleigh

While others lay on the ground

Making angels was fun

A glorious moment in time it is

For it brings memories for me

A joyful childhood it was for me

A golden memory for me

BBQ

You wrap the jumbo shrimp

With applewood bacon

Seasoning steaks for its flavor

Lighting the coals beneath the grill

While waiting for the coals to become hot

You make your homemade BBQ sauce

Pulling the racks of ribs from the pale

You season them as well

You pop the top to your favorite ale

Line your seasonings up on the grill

Now you shuck the husk from the corn

You check the coals

They are hot and ready

You begin to cook slow and steady

Minute by minute you wait

To apply the sauce that taste so great

Your hunger grows strong by the minute

As you smell the aroma of the sauce

Which lingers in the air

Finally the food comes off the grill

Fully cooked and prepared

Lining your plate with your feast

You sit down to the table

And have another drink

You savor the flavor with each bite

Grateful for this wonderous delight

You finish your meal

With a slice of pie

Graced with homemade ice cream on the side

Brings the smile of total delight

About the Author:

Paul Randall Fox (Highway), is a writer of poems, poetry, short stories, and novels. Paul has a unique style for, video poetry, photo poetry. Some of his writings, and poetry can be found displayed on:

Facebook: @Highways Feelings

Instagram: @highways feelings

Made in the USA
Las Vegas, NV
20 March 2022

46022526R00059